M000187657

N. Pr
keep dreaming
BIG!

DREAMERS, TAKE ACTION!

The blueprint to go from dreamer to doer

NIKKIE PRYCE

Copyright © 2017 Nikkie Pryce

All rights reserved. No part of this publication may be reproduced, distributed, or transmitted in any form or by any means, including photocopying, recording, or other electronic or mechanical methods, without the prior written permission of the publisher, except in the case of brief quotations embodied in critical reviews and certain other noncommercial uses permitted by copyright law.

ISBN 13: 978-1-945532-28-3

ISBN: 1-945532-28-9

Published by Opportune Independent Publishing Company

Cover Design by Live Life Creative

Printed in the United States of America

For permission requests, write to the publisher, addressed "Attention: Permissions Coordinator" to the address below.

Email: Npryce.info@gmail.com

DEDICATION

To my Lord and Savior Jesus Christ.
Thank you for pushing me to "finish."

To my mother, Naomi Morrison (1964–2016)
I honor you with the work of my hands. This one is for
you. Here's to us "finishing" with aggressive faith.

-Nikkie Pryce

CONTENTS

Foreword

Growing up in the Pentecostal church, I've witnessed various ways to acknowledge when God is using someone to minister to my situation.

I can:
   A. Wave my hand so that the preacher knows I'm a witness.
   B. Yell "Amen" while waving my hand from the comfort of my seat.
   C. Stand up, point at the preacher and yell "amen."
   D. Throw the closest piece of fabric I can find at the preacher so that he/she knows God is speaking directly to me.
   E. All of the above.

The answer is "E. All of the above."

No matter your religious or spiritual beliefs, *Dreamers, Take Action!* is for every person who inhales and exhales. If you are alive, you can dream.

This text took me on a journey. At first, I thought this course was about Nikkie Pryce, but a few pages into this book, I realized that this expedition was about my dreams.

In "Step 1: Dreamers' Insomnia," I was convicted. After wiping the crust out of my eyes, I was able to see long enough to recognize that I have been sleeping on my gifts.

Thank God for friends like Nikkie who hold me accountable. She once sent me a text to remind me of the call on my life: "Quit playing, bro...that gift isn't just for you, GA. When you finish what God asked you to finish, blessings will come."

If I had not read her message in public, I would have crawled into a corner and cried, but I couldn't do that. I had to own my mistakes. I had to own my insomnia and challenge myself to push through my fears and anxiety. "It's going to bless everyone around you," she told me. I read her message in the voice of God. It was as if the Father, Son and Holy Ghost came down from heaven and surrounded me.

This was an intervention.

While we were classmates at Florida A&M University, it wasn't until six years later that our friendship matured. In the words of Nikkie's late mother, "People need people." The funny thing is I never knew I needed her until she showed up.

You see, she challenges me. This book is a piece of Nikkie's heart. Not the cute heart you learn to draw in first grade… the bleeding flesh you turn away from while watching a heart transplant on Grey's Anatomy.

An organ transplant is nothing to take lightly; It saves lives.

Nikkie, your words have awakened my gifts and I pray that every dreamer reading this foreword dreams with the same fire that you have ignited in me.

throws handkerchief at altar

Georgia Dawkins
Television producer and author of Too Dope Queens (blog series)

Acknowledgments

How could I write this book without the many sacrifices people have made for me? The late-night conversations, advice and compassion; it was all appreciated. To my mother, Naomi Morrison—thank you for reminding me to put God before everything. My father, Garfield Pryce —thank you for being one of my biggest support systems. I'm not sure where I would be without you two.

To my siblings, Kareen, Andrae and Tiffany—I am grateful that God thought enough of us to put us together. Love you guys.

To my cousin who is almost like my sister, Tass—we are so much alike in more ways than one. Thank you for praying my way through this thing called life. I love you.

To my cousin Tracy. My God, you're a wonder! You've stretched your arms for me through this process, along with Ty, Torie, Tyler and Benie. This process was made easier because of the love you guys showed me. May blessings overflow your lives.

To my aunties, who somehow turned into my second

mothers. Auntie Claudette, Auntie Pat and Auntie Bev. Thank you for always praying my way through.

To my best friend Farraw—whenever I think of you, I remember how much God loves me. Thank you for loving me unconditionally through this entire process.

To Celest—my mentor but most of all my big sister. Thank you for always being an answer.

To Marcus Rosier—if it weren't for your sensitivity this book wouldn't have gotten started. Thank you.

To my family members, friends and loved ones far and wide—I appreciate you. Each of you has been a part of my growth. Thank you for simply loving me through it all.

To my organization, The I AM Community—I am so thankful for your creation. Thank you to all of our members. Life wouldn't make sense without you!

Lastly, I acknowledge you—the one reading this book right now. You're going to make a difference, if you work hard. You're going to get the life you want, if you're disciplined. You got this!

INTRODUCTION

"Don't give up. Finish what you've started."

That's so hard to say, especially coming from a person like me. I've rarely ever finished anything that I've pursued in my life.

However, this time it is different.

I finished this assignment to create a life for the both of us. "Us" being the dreamers who have so much inside of our mind, body and soul, but were barely taught to manifest it to completion.

On my journey of being a dreamer, I realized that one thing was wrong: I was too busy dreaming, starting amazing ideas but not finishing the things I dreamt about.

Today, I pass down what I've learned. I pass down what I've encountered during this journey in hopes that you will use this book as a tool to not make the same mistakes that I made. Instead, use it to learn and reroute yourself onto the path to your success. I trust your ability just like I trust mine. Take this journey with me and let's conquer together. We owe it to ourselves, and we only can imagine where it will take us.

The goal is to not get distracted for any reason. Focus on your dream and vision 1000%. Most importantly, don't give up. Finish what you've started, just like I've finished this book! It took some time, prayer and focus, but we are here.

Let me show you how I did it. After this, pay it forward. Share your journey with all around you so each of us can learn from each other and not make the same mistakes twice.

STEP ONE

DREAMERS' INSOMNIA

I want to be the first to congratulate you! You have recognized the need to improve your process of execution, and are taking steps towards doing so.

First and foremost, you've opened this book. Probably to your surprise, and smack dab in the middle of this page, you instantly saw the words "Dreamers' Insomnia." Crazy isn't it? Well, this chapter is one that will open your eyes—literally.

To explain, dreamers are always alert and ready. We are far too busy dreaming and formulating plans, ideas and concepts for taking ourselves to the next level. Seriously, how could one sleep when there is so much to do?

Now, I know at this point you're taking the term "sleep" as in the act of your eyes being closed, your muscles relaxed and your mind counting several sheep. But when I speak on "sleeping," I actually mean being physically awake, but watching your dreams pass you by. Every single day, watching someone doing the very thing that you love while you fall "asleep" on your talent, skill and dreams.

It's time to snap out of it now, my dear. Wake up! Now is the time to awaken from that comatose state and get started. Now, luckily for you, I'm here to push you. Why, you ask? Why do I care to do this? Simple. You deserve this, just like I did.

I was the same dreamer, watching as potential passed me by. I made excuses for not creating my life because of the fear of success. After a lot of self-talk and affirmations, which lifted my self-esteem and motivation, I stopped making excuses and I put in the work. We are a team, and your success in this is the key to our future.

You have so much untapped potential, and unless you develop a case of Dreamers' Insomnia when it comes to pursuing your dreams, we will never make it. I need you as much as you need me. You have literally everything inside of you to make this happen, if you allow it.

The symptoms of insomnia are difficulty falling asleep, having trouble going back to sleep and waking up too early in the morning. Wouldn't it make a world of difference if you had the same exact symptoms for chasing your dreams?

Wouldn't it feel amazing if you said, "I wake up too early. I have difficulty falling asleep. I have trouble going back to sleep because I'm too busy working towards my dreams?" If you've ever felt any of these symptoms, I am officially diagnosing you with D.I. (Dreamers' Insomnia).

Curtis "50 Cent" Jackson, one of the most successful and prominent businessmen in the hip-hop and entertainment industry, left a lasting impression when he was filming on a movie set.

The question was asked, "50 when do you sleep?" His response was nothing short of brilliant: "Sleep? Sleep is for those people who are broke. I don't sleep, I might miss the opportunity to make a dream become a reality."

This remarkable answer has been stuck in my head since the first time I heard it. To me, it represents the ultimate example of a *doer*. He has chosen to prioritize opportunities over basic human needs. This may seem drastic, and maybe was not even meant literally, but he has a real understanding of not letting opportunities pass by.

Just think about it: How many opportunities have we missed because we were unprepared or simply waiting? Be it waiting for the right time to do something, or waiting for whatever it is that's keeping us from doing.

When you're fully engaged on pursuing your dreams and wanting to see them manifest, sleep will be a thing of the past—whether that's a physical or mental interpretation. Through this book I will show you how I developed D.I., and how you can do the same and put it to use. Through these steps, you'll awaken a mindset you never knew you had.

WHAT KEEPS YOU UP AT NIGHT?

What keeps you tossing and turning in the middle of the night? What's that burning sensation deep in your body that says, "I need to do this, now!"

We don't have to take that term literally, but if you've lost sleep, stayed up for long hours, and sacrificed friends, relationships and occasional outings with your buddies in order to chase this dream, then it's definitely something worth pursing. If you can sacrifice your personal life and give every ounce of thought to this dream, then why haven't you moved your feet yet?

It's now August 30, 2015, at 2:18 a.m., and finishing this book is all that I can think about. Over the years, I've had such a hard time simply finishing. Ideas would come to me instantly. I would even get started on most of them, but I could never finish any of them. It's not that I didn't want to, it's that I didn't develop the discipline and work ethic that it took to finish.

When this book idea came to me, it never dawned on me that the next 30 days of my life would be so crucial. I set a plan to have this done within a month. I thought to myself, *How can I finish this in 30 days?* I had a hard time focusing on anything for 30 minutes.

But, I knew there would be many sleepless nights, all while working a full-time job that required my time five days out of the week. Every day that I woke up to go to work reminded me of the importance of challenging myself to finish this. Not only was this critical for me to finally complete something, but I knew this book would get into the hands of the dreamer who would need this years from now.

So, I sacrificed instant gratification to make sure this tool got into your hands. My hope is that you'll sacrifice many nights, as well, to help the person who will need you in the future.

WHAT DOES BEING PASSIONATE MEAN?

Passionate is defined by dictionary.com as, "Expressing or showing intense or strong feeling." It goes beyond having an ambitious nature; it means materializing and visualizing that vision & putting it into action. Typically when someone is passionate, they will give every ounce of blood, sweat and tears to see something come into fruition.

I believe the biggest question isn't *if* we have passion, but *why* aren't we going after what we are passionate about? Seriously, what is the hold up? Is it the fear of failure? Is it fear of security? Is it the fear that this may actually work? Is it that we've allowed laziness to suck the life out of us like a leech does to its host?

If we really sat down for a moment and answered those questions, who would really want to live like that? Well, for starters I know you don't. If you did, you wouldn't be engaging and using this tool. In reality, you're a whole lot closer than you think you are.

My passion for finishing came from working in an industry where I wasn't fulfilled. Granted, I created the lifestyle I wanted. I lived in one of the best living spaces in the city, I had money in the bank, and I could buy any designer that I pleased. But I wasn't at all happy.

I wanted to do something that made me feel purposeful. Even though I am grateful for the experience, the money simply wasn't enough for me. I needed to live on purpose. I needed to help someone become the best version of themselves. I needed to create *Dreamers, Take Action!*

FIND WHAT YOU LOVE

When you awaken every morning, what's the first thought that crosses your mind? How do you connect yourself with family, friends and people that you love? Do you get joy from the birth of a child being brought into this world?

Does your heart swell with joy when you've given to someone financially, even if it's your last dime? I have so much faith in your ability to think back into your life's memories and locate those moments. We are so blessed to experience "moments" in our lives.

Times that connect us to people, situations and glorious periods that made us feel warm, whole and significant. Pay close attention to the "moments" that you encounter. Be still and embrace exactly what it is that you're feeling. When the breeze is blowing, when a small child kisses you on the cheek or when someone is pouring encouragement into your life, those are the times to feel inspired and pinpoint what you love and awakens your passion.

Use these times to recall at what point in your life you felt valued. Whether someone gave you something or you gave to someone else, what did that moment feel like to you? Close your eyes, take a deep breath and be present in that moment. In these specific instances is how we find what we love. The feeling that we felt from that moment has brought us to our "now."

I remember when I was 14 years old and a cheerleader. I would often leave to go and assist the younger squad with their movements. I wanted to make sure their legs were correctly positioned, their arms where straight and they were saying all the correct words to their cheers.

Even though I risked being scolded for leaving my squad, I saw a need and couldn't leave them out in the cold. Interestingly enough, to this day, I can recall that I didn't do it out of the need for perfection, but because my heart saw a need for someone younger and smaller than I was.

They had all the passion in the world to be great. They just needed a little push. As I've gotten older, I understand that I've always had a passion to help others. My heart is big and full of love and compassion for people. I found my love of helping people reach their maximum potential by reflecting on those small moments from my past.

So now it's your turn. Think of a time when you did something that made you feel full and captivated. By doing so, you can find what you love. It's time to ask yourself those familiar questions, "What am I good at? What drives me to take action? How can I help make someone's situation better?

What do I have to offer someone else that can take them to the next level? When you start to reach from your heart and apply the answers to these questions, you can finally get the answers you're looking for. It's as simple as asking yourself, "What do I love?"

DIE EMPTY

This section, I believe, is the game-changer. Those two words are eight letters filled with so much impact. Repeat after me, "When I die, I must die empty." We've been granted a life on this earth. One life. With a limited amount of time. No one knows when they will be called home.

No man or woman has a countdown clock that says, "You're coming up on your final days. Get ready!" But, imagine if we did have this. Fathom the thought of actually knowing when your last day would be. What would you really do to make a difference while you're still here?

Would you create a formula that can prevent the transmission of diseases? Would you invent an airplane that can maneuver through the sky without wings? Would you write the book that you know you were supposed to write years ago? Would you call your ill grandmother whom you haven't spoken to in God knows how long?

Would you reach out to a friend that you've hurt over something meaningless? What would you do if you knew when you would take your last breath? There is always one thing that is for sure—death is inevitable.

We are all aware of that. But you have a very significant gift in your possession. The gift of NOW. So let's think, what are you doing right now that is setting up your future? When it's your time, you should have emptied out all of your creativity, brilliance, ideas, projects and inventions.

There's a scripture that I refer to from time to time. It keeps me abreast and alert to always create and never stop. Genesis 1:28 (KJV) states that we should be fruitful (bring forth good works, bring forth good fruit), multiply, replenish and dominate.

These commands were given to us since the beginning of time. We are given this home and this body for such a short time. It's a privilege to have this life, knowing many people didn't make it this far. What are your plans to change not only your circumstance, but every single person's life as well?

Todd Henry, author of the book *Die Empty, Unleash Your Best Work Every Day*, wrote something so profound that if I didn't quote it, I don't believe I would be able to effectively express it in my own words. He said, "This begs the obvious question: How do you set in motion a course of action that will allow you to unleash your best, most valuable work, while you still can?" This should be a question that ignites the fire inside of your soul. That burning passion that says, "While you still can, what will you do next?"

This chapter impacts me so much because on July 24, 2016, I experienced death firsthand. My mother passed away from cancer. I watched her take her last breath as she fought a great battle against that dreadful disease. My mother was the strongest woman I've ever met in my life. She was first diagnosed with Crohn's disease in the late '90s.

According to Mayo Clinic, *Crohn's disease is a chronic inflammatory bowel disease that affects the lining of the digestive tract.* My mom fought through Crohn's, and in 2015, she was diagnosed with stage two cancer. Being the fighter that my mom was, she beat it and went into remission.

A few months later, cancer showed its ugly face again. This time, worse—she was in stage four. However, she proudly went to her chemotherapy sessions, and with my siblings and I supporting her, she fought this fight without complaining.

I watched my mom confess her faith to other patients as we entered the doors for her therapy. It was the hardest time of my life, as it was extremely difficult to see my mother go through this process. But, she did it and never gave up. I remember her saying, "God is taking care of me."

On July 23, 2016, my mother had been nonresponsive for a few days. We were alerted the night before, from the hospice nurse, that she may not make it through the night. On that Sunday morning of July 24, I woke up with my sister and brother sleeping next to my mother.

We decided to surround her as she slept through the night. I went to the bathroom at approximately 7:30 a.m. When I returned, she was still breathing yet remained silent. All I could hear was the oxygen pump running as she inhaled and exhaled.

I sat down behind her and played Tasha Cobbs' album, *One Place Live*, for her. Around 9:30 a.m. I literally saw my mom take her last breath. I alerted my family and watched her face, which was the most peaceful sight I've ever seen. My mom won this battle. God kept his promise. He healed her.

My mom lived by two words: *aggressive faith*. She kept her faith through this process and never gave up. She fulfilled her purpose on this earth. If you learn anything from this book, learn to keep pushing forward, even when it gets tough. The times when you want to give up are exactly the times when your greatest miracle is around the corner.

Stick to it for just a bit longer. Let my mom's life be your example. Live out loud. Dream anyway. Finish strong. Keep your aggressive faith. Most important, when it's time, die empty.

At the end of each chapter you'll find challenges. These are strategies I took when life got rough.

There were times I started to miss my mom or something just wasn't working out for me, and I needed an outlet. I used each challenge to boost my self-confidence and increase my positive energy. As a result, I was in a great mood and could conquer my day. I hope each challenge encourages you when you have tough days. Be reminded to keep pressing forward and know that all is working out for you.

Dreamers Action Challenge #1:

This challenge will inspire you to dig deep. You will find what you love and are passionate about.

What you will need:
- A 12 oz. glass mason jar with lid
- 10–15 small pieces of paper about 1.5"x 2" in size (you can cut this from a larger piece of construction or loose-leaf paper)
- A pen
- Any assortment of alphabetical letters in sticker form
- Colorful ribbon for decoration (optional)

What you will do:
After you have all supplies, decorate the outside of the jar with the stickers and ribbon. I normally tie the ribbon around the rim of the jar where the lid is connected.

You can use your stickers on the outside of the jar to give the jar a name. My jar is called my *Love and Passion Jar*. You can call it whatever you'd like, pertaining to finding what you love and what you're passionate about.

Fill the 16 oz. mason jar with the small pieces of paper.

On each piece of paper for 10 days, you'll write what made you feel passionate that day. What did you fall in love with on that day? Did you help an elderly lady get on the elevator?

Did you help a child walk up the stairs? Did you give money to the homeless? Did you encourage a young girl going through a tough time in life? Well, if you did any of those things, write it on the sheets of paper and close the lid of the jar.

Repeat this exercise for the next 10 days. At the end of the 10 days, open the jar and read your entries. What patterns do you see? Out of everything that was written do you see patterns of thoughtfulness? Selflessness? Kindness? Leadership? Sincerity? What sticks out the most to you?

That's where we will start first. Out of all of your entries, find one word that connects all of your good deeds together. Write it at the end of this chapter on the space below. That's where your love, heart and passion lie—from that one word.

STEP TWO

DREAMERS AWAKEN

Now, by this chapter, you should've awakened from your slumber and started seeing your life from a new perspective. Through this tool, *Dreamers, Take Action!*, I hope you feel as though you've gotten a fresh start and you are on the right path.

Now that I have your new and improved attention, let me start by saying this chapter will begin by challenging you to think. Yes, I said it. Use that magnificent God-given brain that you have to stretch your very existence.

You've learned what you're passionate about and what you love. Now, we will dig a little deeper. You're here for a reason. The reason you've been given breath in your body, to even be able to read this book, is because you have purpose on your life.

From my own personal gatherings, purpose simply means your intent for being in this world. What are you supposed to be doing while you're here?

Sounds pretty exciting, right? Well, when you're trying to find what it is you were created to do, it's the least bit exciting; it's frightening, confusing and worrisome. I felt all of those feelings before I understood what I am here for.

I used to stay up at night questioning myself, *What are you here for?* It took years for me to tap into the answer. To be honest with you, the answer was within me all along. I started to read more, and one of my favorite books that helped with this process was *The Purpose Driven Life* by Rick Warren.

It gave me practical steps to understanding my purpose and what I was created for. I used to journal about what made me feel fulfilled and what brought certainty and absoluteness to my very being. I also listened when others talked to me. Even when I was at the lowest places in my life, I still helped others.

I remember going through a horrible breakup in college. I was so depressed and sad that it had ended. I literally cried myself to sleep every night. One night my phone rang. As I answered, my co-worker at the time was on the line begging to see and speak with me.

I jumped out of bed, found a pair of sweatpants, a baggy t-shirt and my college hooded sweater. I ran downstairs into my car and drove to a restaurant not too far from my apartment where we had agreed to meet. As I entered the restaurant, there she was, crying, sad and miserable.

She was going through a death in her family. Instantly,

I straightened up, forgot about my issues and consoled her in complete silence. We didn't say a word, and I believe my positive energy, which seemed to come out of nowhere, was imparted to her.

After some time, she hugged and thanked me. From that moment, I realized I had found my purpose. I am here to uplift, inspire and motivate others to be their best selves. Out of all this, the most important revelation was that I needed to take care of myself as well.

I needed to cater to my heart and love on myself constantly, so when it's time to be there for someone else, I'm not depleted and wounded so badly from my own bad choices. From that day forward, I finally got it. I knew one day that I would make a difference in this world. I didn't want to just exist, nor was I willing to obtain power, glory or praise without using it to help others.

I remember finishing college and working for a local news station in the city I resided in at the time. I started working as a news editor. My responsibility was to edit all of the video for the sunrise morning show.

My part-time shift was from 2 a.m.–7 a.m., and then it was time to head to my full-time second job, a rental car shop not too far from the station, to work an 8 a.m.–5 p.m. shift. I completed the same routine over and over, for five days out of the week.

I did that for about six months too long. It had to be the longest, most strenuous six months known to man. At least I felt that way. But, I was committed. Surprisingly, after six months I was promoted to digital content editor at the station. My job was to add content and stories to the website. This was a lot easier than editing video and I was beyond thankful for the opportunity, but still something didn't feel right.

I don't know about anyone else, but I talk to myself from time to time. It's just my thing. I remember saying, "Nikkie, don't complain. It's not what you want but it's what you have, so be grateful." So, I did what I had to do.

Two weeks after that, I was promoted again, but this time to co-host a show on our sister network. Now, this was a dream come true. So many sensations lingered through my body, as I felt I was doing exactly what I thought I should be doing.

This finally felt like my moment.

Since elementary school, I always knew I was supposed to do something on television. I just didn't know what. When I was chosen to do the morning announcements at school, my fifth grade teacher told me something that I'll never forget. She said, "No matter what you do or where you go in life, this is your calling. Do this."

I will forever be grateful for her saying that, but if you can imagine, at the time my first thought was, *Seriously, lady? What does "do this" mean?* Well, 10 years later, I was about to find out how it was all connected to my purpose.

Fast forward, to when I was fresh out of college and co-hosting the TV show. My responsibility was to get the reactions of our social media followers on major world topics and report them live on-air. This was a really neat opportunity and I was beyond grateful, but there was still something missing.

I know I sound like the spoiled brat who isn't grateful and is never satisfied, but please bear with me while I explain. Each day, walking into the station, I still had to update the site and co-host on the show. There are stories out there that can't be released on air because of the graphic nature.

Sometimes, it would break my heart to hear the things that were happening around the world. I remember reading a story of some teens committing a horrendous crime against one another. It's just too graphic to go into detail.

I often asked myself, *Where did they learn this stuff?* But it was their reality, and as most people in the industry would tell me, *after a while, you'll become used to it.* How could someone get used to reading stories like that every single day? From that moment, I knew reporting news stories to that capacity wasn't for me. But what could I do in order to change this?

A few weeks later, I put in my two weeks' notice.

I wanted to find out what was next for me. Where was I supposed to be going next? I left and never turned back. Was that the best decision that I could've made? At the time, and for the sake of my dreams, absolutely.

However, there was an apartment where rent was required, which I now had no money to pay for. So, due to my career liberation, two months later I was kicked out of my apartment and forced to live with some friends for the next year.

After sleeping on the couch for the first few weeks, I was able to move into one of the rooms there. Trust me, in that moment it was a whole lot better than sleeping on the couch. But I remember feeling worthless, miserable and foolish. I left stability for a dream? Who does that? A person who believes in themselves. The most successful people know they will make a way out of no way.

Reality finally kicked in, when I was without a job, without an apartment and the only possessions I had were my clothes and my vehicle. I wanted to change what I saw and start living out my purpose, but I had no clue how to do that. I was so angry and upset. I felt like my world was crashing down on me.

But I had to figure this out. I needed to find a way to connect with my purpose so I could help others. I always knew that my gifts and talents would create a life for me, but I was missing a simple step: consistent and undeniable action.

During that lonely time, I started taking action. I read a lot—the Bible, stories about life and purpose and self-help books. Most importantly, I meditated. That opened up so much peace for me during this transition. It showed me my true self when I connected with my higher self. It was the most liberating process of action that I could have ever taken. It was the start to my new beginning.

HOW DOES PASSION CONNECT TO PURPOSE?

This morning I went to the restroom to get my day started. You know, the typical daily routine we all commit to: Take a shower, brush your teeth and get dressed. Sounds about right.

Well, I only use one brand of toothpaste. Of course, this complements my obsessive compulsive disorder (that I haven't been diagnosed with, but something has to explain my constant need of having things a particular way). I only use Sensodyne Extra Whitening toothpaste.

On this day, as I spread it over the bristles of my toothbrush, I began to brush my teeth and glance at the back of the tube.

On one line it read "active ingredients," and on the same line it read "purpose." I thought to myself, *Why would they add the word "purpose" to a tube of toothpaste? Aha!* (In my best Oprah impersonation). This was one of those "aha" moments for me.

According to dictionary.com, *purpose is the reason for which something exists or is done, made, used, etc.*

The active ingredients were added to make the toothpaste more effective, but without those ingredients, the toothpaste couldn't serve its purpose. As with you, my friend, without your passion, gifts, and talents (your ingredients) you wouldn't be able to make a difference in this world (serve your purpose).

If a tube of toothpaste is created to serve a purpose then you were certainly created to do something big and life-changing. Connect what you're passionate about to your purpose, give of yourself, and just like those active ingredients, do what you were created to do.

BE COMPELLED TO MAKE A DIFFERENCE

I don't believe the question is, *What are you passionate about?* The real question is, *What moves you?* If you saw something happening, what would make you want to change it for the better? What evokes such a feeling in you that you desire to make a difference?

My emotions stemmed from seeing my sister not have the best situations handed to her in life. She was very sad most of her adolescent years when our parents divorced, followed by having a child at a young age. But regardless of her tough circumstances, my sister is filled with so many gifts that she has yet to embrace.

When I was in college as a student reporter, every night I would go home and talk to her about her day and issues that affected her. An idea for a news story would always develop from our conversations, so I brought them up to my class the next day. I would get an "A" on every story!

Not to mention, when I was doing freelance hosting at different events, I would be nervous out of my mind, and she would gently say, "Nikkie, just be yourself." From just hearing that, I would do the best job I'd ever done at any of my shows.

There's such a power and stillness in her voice to speak into the lives of others. She isn't a woman of many words, but when she does speak, it compels. Admittedly, I wouldn't have been successful at some of my projects without her words.

However, I always knew my sister deserved more, but it was up to her to go get it. If only I could make her see the world that awaits her if she didn't settle. It moved my heart to gain the success I had, but also to help my sister achieve her own.

I was compelled. Not only by my sister, but every other person out there who wants more but simply doesn't feel good enough to go get it.

My passion has always been to encourage and help others. After experiencing the numerous amount of people who have dreams but don't feel like they are enough to go for it, I had to figure out a way to change this mindset. From there, my purpose unfolded right before my eyes. My purpose bloomed like a bouquet of bright red roses.

My purpose spoke to me. It said, "Teach people how to make it happen. Not just for themselves, but for everyone else around them." Instantly, a light came on! I've developed a heart for the group of people who simply just couldn't figure it out. Who couldn't even form what they love into words, much less take action on it.

<u>CLARITY</u>

I believe clarity is needed in every situation. From my point of view, there is only black and white. No gray areas can exist when it comes to having clarity. You have to be certain and secure. To begin with the process of clarity, there has to be a conversation of expectations.

What is it that you want? Have a self-assessment and ask, "Am I 100% clear on the things that I desire?" You can have whatever it is that you want. Listen, if you want it, it's yours.

Speak what you want and expect everything that you've asked for to become subject to your very voice. The first step consists of saying what you want, then expecting it to come into fruition. Of course, you have to put the work in as well to see it happen.

I used to believe that I was too spoiled, that my standards and expectations were too much to ask anyone for. But that was a lie. Now I live my life on the terms of whatever it is I want, I will have.

If it didn't turn out how I intended it to, I knew God had something better waiting for me. I had to become so clear and precise with what I wanted. I could no longer second-guess myself and what I desired. When expressed, some people would think that I was asking for too much. That wasn't the case.

We just have different perspectives, which is totally

alright. We're different people with different thoughts and emotions. But, I was aware of everything I wanted and needed in this life and was destined to receive it at any cost.

I wasn't leaving this earth without getting everything I was promised by God. It was mine and that's all that mattered.

Don't be afraid of rejection—continue on the path of having the clear vision that you desire. It's yours, so just go after it and never ever settle. No matter what.

Here are a few practical principles that you can apply to get the necessary desired outcome that you expect:

1. Have a healthy look at yourself. Have you put yourself in the position to have the things that you want? Have you taken the time to commit to self-care and self-love? Have you done for yourself all the things that you're requesting from a spouse, career or family member? Most importantly, evaluate yourself first to start receiving what you're asking for.

2. Your next step includes having a talk with yourself about desired goals and the necessary steps that need to be taken to get what you want. Close your eyes. Take a moment to visualize exactly what it is that you want. Embrace what that actually looks like. Even if the visual seems insane and unrealistic, accept what you're visualizing. Let it become a part of your norm.

3. Next, set priorities. You will have to define a strict and structured way to prioritize what's most important to you at this current stage in your life. This is the most valuable set of instructions because this is where you make a decision. Do you party and hang out carelessly, or do you stay in and finish the assignment? A decision has to be made of where you are and where you want to be. Hanging out and being the life of the party will always be there. Use this time to better yourself and your situation.

Currently, it's September 20, 2015, at 2:38 a.m. I can't sleep. Writing has kept me up for the past several nights. I forget to have a meal most nights. My entire being is being poured into this book. I've been stretched in my thoughts, vocabulary, reading, time management skills and perspective on what I can accomplish. I have rarely finished anything in my life. To even fathom that this book is almost finished being written is life-changing.

Want to see who you really are? Discipline yourself for a short time. Let's say 30 days. Commit to starting and finishing something. I can guarantee who you really are will come forward. After dedicating myself to finishing this book, I value my time so much more now.

I no longer waste my time on people and situations that don't grow me as a person. I guess it's because I didn't waste time on this project. It was like something inside of me changed, and now I value myself in a whole different way.

There's so much on my mind that I want to tell you. Of

course, there are other things that I wish I could be doing, like counting sheep until I'm off to Slumber Street and Dream Avenue. However, I have to be so definite about what's happening right now.

My tunnel vision has to be on 1000. There are a lot of great concepts and creative ideas that I've come up with and often pursued, but out of so many "great ideas" I can't say that I took the time to reach the destination of finalizing the vision.

So now there's this huge assignment in front of me that I believe is bigger than me. There has to be a strict disciplined place of focus. Your focal point on finishing has to be so accurate and absolute that it's mind-blowing.

For a short time you'll have to give up some things. Sometimes, that consists of friends and family. This may be difficult, but it's possible and necessary. During this time, I was never available. Seriously, no one could get in touch with me because I was so tuned in to what I was doing.

I literally went to work and would go straight home to write. I did this for 30 days straight, every single day. This may have been a bit drastic, but I tend to occasionally experience the "shiny object syndrome."

You know, you fall in love with one shiny object then another one comes along, and immediately you drop that one for this one. Yeah, I had to break that habit, and I did it by getting focused. I had to cut, purge and immediately remove anything that stood in the way of my execution.

I had to block calls and stop answering the phone and get focused. I couldn't miss this. I had too much to do. Listen, it's alright to know that not everyone can go on this journey with you. Most times, you have to go alone and bring others back with you when you make it.

At other times, some people need to be cut off indefinitely. Don't look back, or you may just turn to a pillar of salt like Lot's wife in the story of Sodom and Gomorrah in the Bible. Time to get focused and gain the clarity needed to execute.

Dreamers Action Challenge #2:

This challenge consists of writing the vision. I used this challenge to gain clarity on all the things that I wanted and prayed for. I hope it encourages you to write the vision and see it happen.

What you will need:
- A pen
- Your journaling notebook

What you will do:
In your notebook, write these three questions:
1. What am I good at?
2. What could I see myself doing for free, if I had to?
3. What brings me the most joy?

In detail, write your answers to each question.

Use some time to meditate on your answers. Take some alone time to figure out how you'll apply your answers to your everyday life. This is the beginning of gaining clarity on your purpose.

Step Three

DREAMERS THINK BIG!

One thing I know as a fact is that dreamers do not have the capacity to think small. Their minds have been stretched to believe that small is no longer an option. American physician, poet and professor Oliver Wendell Holmes said it best, "A mind that has been stretched by a new experience cannot go back to its original dimension."

Let me explain a little more. I've worked in the luxury timepiece industry. Before working there, I had an idea of what luxury was, but that was quickly changed by being exposed to a new level of it.

To define it, luxury is the state of great comfort and extravagant living. Originally, I thought an expensive timepiece was a couple of hundred dollars and that the average person would never spend more than that on one. Well, once I started working within this industry I experienced clients spending more than $60k on a watch.

Initially it was shocking, but after a while, it became

my norm. Now, my mind has been stretched to a new idea of luxury. I've been exposed to a lifestyle that many have known all of their lives. It's as if the blinders were removed from my eyes and I could finally see. How'd I get this opportunity to be exposed to a new truth?

I could've easily settled for a 9 to 5 that paid well and offered a few benefits here and there, but my thinking was different.

I didn't have a bad childhood, and my parents lived comfortably for most of their lives. But, the reality that some of my immediate family did not have enough (whether that was money or resources) always caused me to want more out of life.

I always wanted the best that this life had to offer. In my adult life, I wanted to put myself in the position to be in the "right places at the right times." I needed to go where I knew people with a higher status shopped. If I was going to work a corporate job, I would make sure that it fit the lifestyle I wanted.

So, I went on a search to work alongside some of the best in the industry. The day I met my boss, we laughed and joked, and we meshed so well that I was offered a salary package I couldn't refuse.

What if I settled for ordinary? What if I accepted the first opportunity that came my way because I needed a job? I wouldn't have gotten the opportunity to work with celebrities, athletes, surgeons and entrepreneurs.

My thinking "big" made me realize that one day I wanted that life for myself. The smartest thing to do was to position and connect myself with the same type of person that I wanted to be like.

The point is, small thinking won't take you to the next level and beyond. How can you elevate your life if you have the same stagnant mindset as the person you've said you never wanted to be like? Dreamers are always thinking of new ways to evolve so they can help the person behind them evolve as well.

They are sincerely too busy thinking of their next BIG move. Being a big dreamer doesn't mean you aren't focused on your surroundings, or you're oblivious to what's happening around you. It just means you've connected to your higher self.

Our higher selves don't settle for mediocrity. We desire and want the best and we live life to the fullest. You've found your divine purpose and you will reach it at any cost. We've already concluded that you're a dreamer. Putting action behind those dreams will open up doors of opportunity that you would've never imagined.

YOUR THOUGHTS ARE YOUR TRUTH

Close your eyes and inhale and exhale for about five seconds. Next, say one word that describes who you are. That one word describes your truth. Whoever you think you are is exactly who you will be. Thoughts are beyond powerful. They manifest into words, and words manifest into reality. What are you thinking about yourself?

Who do you say you are? What do you believe you deserve? Thoughts are very powerful, but they can also be very dangerous if not used in the right way. If you are reading this book, perhaps you have the same beliefs as I do.

We live in a world with so many different people, ideas, concepts and personalities. I won't assume that we will be on the same page as it relates to how we perceive our faith and understanding. However, there are practices that have proven to have worked in my life.

In the Bible, Habakkuk 2:2 (NIV), there is a verse that says, "Then the Lord replied: Write down the revelation, and make it plain on tablets so that a herald (or so that whoever reads it) may run with it." In other words, write it down, make it plain.

An article in Forbes magazine stated that a study done by Gail Matthews at Dominican University concluded that those who wrote down their goals accomplished significantly more than those who do not write them down.

I moved out of my mother's house about two years ago and found an apartment closer to where I worked. Before I moved in, I searched high and low to find the perfect pad. This had been the first time I lived alone since I was in college, so it needed to be perfect.

I made a list of exactly what I wanted to have in my

apartment. I wrote in concise detail how I wanted my counters and cabinets to look, what parking spots I wanted to park in, the type of leasing agents I wanted to work with, how much I wanted to pay per month, and how much I wanted my electric bill to be—all the way down to the type of neighbors I wanted.

Deep, right? Let's just say this, though: I got every last thing on my list, and more. There's so much power in writing down, and believing, that you can have everything you want and ask for. The atmosphere will align with what you're declaring.

I told you at the beginning of this chapter that your thoughts are your truth. What you think of yourself flows from your heart and mind, which then flows out of your mouth. When you start to speak it, then it becomes your reality.

It becomes the world that you live in. There's a very important exercise that I like to partake in, called positive "I AM" affirmations. I wrote an entire list of positive words that I believe I AM in my journal. Some of my affirmations were: "I AM a game changer, trendsetter, lover of all beautiful things, a light in the world. I AM beautiful, powerful, mind-blowing, loyal, a writer, a speaker, a world traveler."

This all went back to what I thought of myself. Every single day I spoke those words aloud, repeatedly affirming myself and renewing my thoughts in order to remain steadfast on my worth. "I AM more than enough. I deserve the best this world has to offer."

Isn't it refreshing to feel connected with your higher inner self and be able to express things that hold value? No one in this world can validate me or tell me who I AM.

I AM aware of myself and what I have to offer because God reminds me of this. However, it hasn't always been like this for me.

There was once a time when I felt low. I didn't feel beautiful and secure within myself. I was trying to keep up with the Joneses. One thing about trying to keep up with the Joneses, or even the Kardashians, is that if you aren't on that level yet you may end up going bankrupt.

You can't have champagne taste on a beer budget. You have to be who you are and accept where you are in life. I tried to keep up because I wanted the same attention. I wanted to be appreciated and loved. In my mind, the value of material possessions represented my worth.

I thought that I needed more things in order to be seen as valuable. Oh, what a horrible way to live. You'll stress yourself out trying to prove things to people. I had to change my "stinking thinking" and get my mind right, immediately. I was wasting time and money while forfeiting peace of mind to maintain a lifestyle I didn't need.

But how was I going to change my way of thinking about myself? How was I going to create a better life for myself full of peace, hope and love? I prayed hard about the renewal of my mind. I needed to see the value of how important I was to this world.

When I sit and think of the details of my life, how I was created by a perfect God in an imperfect world and how He so strategically created me to fit a unique and intricate design, the thought alone truly blows me away. He put serious thought into choosing my mother's womb to place me in.

He united my mom and dad, and years later, I was born. He thought about the time of year he wanted me to be conceived, the size of my ears, the color of my eyes, my complexion, the way my body is shaped, the specific pitch of my voice, how I fall in love at the sight of a dozen red roses, and how the quirkiest things about me make me different from anyone else.

How such a big God could consider even the smallest details concerning me is unfathomable. So, if God thought so much about me to put so much effort into my creation then I needed to start thinking the same way about myself.

Once I took the time to investigate these amazing possibilities, I never went back to that lowly way of thinking.

It was important that I valued myself and my life. Hey, we only get one life, so it was time for me to take heed to all that I had and start appreciating it. With this newfound revelation, I was able to accept who I am, what I have and what I could do with it.

Let's start thinking of our thoughts as currency. The more you can renew your mind, the more money you can make.

Simple. So, let's say for every positive thought you have you will receive $100 in your account. Every time you have a negative thought that conflicts with your positive thinking, your account is deducted $50.

Start here. Let's see if you can obtain at least $5,000 in earnings by the end of the week. This basically means you need to have a minimum of 10 positive thoughts a day for five days. Sounds pretty feasible, right? In no time, you'll be on your way to the land of positive thinking, all by working on your mind and creating a new head space to live in.

You are your thoughts. Your thoughts are your currency. It's time to get wealthy.

FEAR IS NOT REAL

"Fear is the most subtle and destructive of all human diseases."

—Dr. Smiley Blanton

Fear is not real. It doesn't exist. We create an image in our own mind that says we should be afraid, fear the outcome and keep ourselves restrained from the truth. The truth of the fact is that we are absolutely brilliant, talented, dynamic and a chosen people.

At times, we've allowed fear to creep in like a silent thief in the night. But in reality, fear doesn't exist. It's a mind thing. Our mind tells us to be scared and afraid of the unknown. Some people may think that if you can't see the expected end, why *shouldn't* you be afraid? Why *shouldn't* you expect for things not to work out in your favor?

There was a very interesting movie called *After Earth,* featuring Will Smith and his son Jaden Smith. It brought into perspective how fear is actually just a thought. It can creep in and ultimately become our reality if we don't stop it in its tracks.

In the movie, Will Smith said, "Fear is not real. The only place that fear can exist is in our thoughts of the future. It is a product of our imagination, causing us to fear things that do not, at present, and may not ever exist. That is near insanity. Do not misunderstand me—danger is very real. But fear is a choice." When you fear, you're telling yourself, the universe and your creator, "I don't trust you." You're basically saying, "I only believe what I see."

Faith is believing, even when you don't see or understand. I want to encourage you to keep going, even if fear creeps in and you are afraid of the outcome of a situation. Do it in fear. 2016 was a life-changing year for me. Not only did I lose my mother that year but I also made some life-changing decisions.

In October 2016, I packed up my beautifully decked-out apartment, put everything into storage, put a leave of absence in to my luxury job and bought a one-way ticket to New York. I was going there only to visit. Little did I know the journey that God was putting me on. When I visited for a week, I fell in love.

The culture, the people, the hustle and bustle, everything. I literally felt like I was given another chance. So, I left everything behind and moved forward. I didn't know what awaited me in NY.

The reality was I could've stayed in Atlanta, comfortable at a job that I had once loved but had lost my flame for. I wanted more. Lo and behold, NY was it. This place wasn't in my plans. I wanted to go to Texas with all of the growing and inspiring young professionals.

What's the saying? "We plan, God laughs." Not to mention I moved in the winter. Wow, I couldn't have possibly been thinking when I made this decision. I was scared out of my wits. I was heading to a place where I had never spent more than a month, and I was leaving everything to go there?

Wait, this can't be right! But I did it. I moved in fear, and immediately the fear started to dissolve. I had family and close friends who uplifted and supported me. This is a testimony that proves fear is not real. In fact, it's the fuel needed to fly the plane and watch your life takeoff.

Dreamers Action Challenge #3:

This challenge consists of writing your positive "I AM" affirmations.

What you will need:
- A pen
- Your journaling notebook
- Your positive thoughts

What you will do:
Grab your notebook and on an entire sheet of paper, write down positive "I AM" affirmations about yourself. You can start with whatever you'd like. For example, I started with, "I AM a writer, giver, trendsetter, leader, lover of life and all beautiful things..."

After your entire sheet is filled with your positive "I AM" affirmations hang it on your wall where it will be visible.

Speak this exercise and repeat every day until it's embedded in your heart and mind. You'll start to feel your self-worth and self-love increase daily.

Dreamers Action Challenge #4:

This challenge consists of jotting down all the positive thoughts you have through the day, paying yourself $100 a day and deducting $50 every time you have a negative thought.

What you will need:

- A pen
- Your journaling notebook or sticky notes
- Your positive thoughts
- A scheduler, planner or reminder application on your smartphone

What you will do:

Start thinking positive thoughts about yourself, your circumstance, your family and your surroundings.

Every time you have a positive thought deposit $100 in your mental memory bank. (You can take note of this in your journaling notebook or on your sticky notes).

Write each positive thought on a sticky note and post somewhere visible around your home (bathroom mirror, living room television, bedroom headboard —make it fun and interesting). Write how much you were paid and your balance on the bottom of the sticky note.

Whenever you have a negative thought, deduct $50 from your account. We won't write the negative thoughts down because they don't matter. Wipe that thought clean and start over. You can do it!

Each day for five days, aim for at least 10 positive thoughts. Add all the numbers together to see where you get. By the end of the week the goal is to have at least $5,000 in the bank. Let's aim to have $20,000 by the end of each month.

By the end of the year you will have earned $240,000 if you consistently had positive thoughts without any deductions.

I knew I was connected to a bunch of rich people! Let's keep it going!

Note: This strategy is to help develop a way to combat negative thoughts. Empower yourself through this method; This strategy has helped me tremendously to pursue and maintain positive thoughts on a daily basis.

STEP FOUR

DREAMERS ARE LEADERS

"Don't waste your time in the race looking back to see where the other guy is or what the other guy is doing. It's not about the other guy. It's about what can you do. You just need to run that race as hard as you can. You need to give it everything you've got, all the time, for yourself."

—Oprah Winfrey

As a dreamer, you are automatically a leader and embody everything that comes with it. You run the pack. You're a trendsetter. People follow your concepts, ideas, lifestyle, even down to the way you dress.

Your social media page is clicked on just for others to admire all of your pictures. But what makes you so special? Why do you stand out from the crowd? It's simple.

You're a leader. Leaders can't blend in, even if they try. You could disguise yourself in sheep's clothing and would still be noticed. You stick out like a sore thumb.

You don't fit in. I'm here to let you know that it is totally alright. It's actually a great problem to have.

Close your eyes, take a deep breath and accept the calling. You were born to stand out. Your ambitious nature and consistent work ethic prove that you're on a whole different level from your counterparts.

How refreshing it is to be reassured that you aren't going insane? I'm here to affirm the feelings you've always had about yourself. Now that you've accepted the calling, we can move forward to the most life-changing revelation. This will bless you real good, if you let it.

How can you lead if you're always watching your opponent? This is a major key in this chapter.

The one way to always avoid being paralyzed by comparison is to remember the only real competition that you have in this world is you. Every day when you wake up, you should ask yourself, "What can I do better today that I didn't do yesterday?"

If you're too concerned about your opponent's every move, you will miss every opportunity that you could've implemented to be a better version of yourself. I constantly repeat to myself, "Don't watch others' blessings so much that you may be missing out on your own. Focus on yourself."

In all honesty and truth, this walk may be one that you take on your own. I'm not suggesting that you don't have mentors, friends or family who are on speed dial, if necessary.

However, it's said that it gets cold at the top. I've experienced this feeling one too many times. There have been people I've had to release and relationships I had to dismiss in order to get the prize at the end.

While writing this book, I've realized the tremendous value of my time. I don't have any desire in the world to waste it ever again. You should look at your time the same exact way. Time is something you will never get back, so always be sure to use it properly and effectively. When a situation or circumstance is a waste of my time I cut it off immediately.

Why in the world would I waste my time on something that I didn't need, or probably didn't want? Wasting time is unnecessary and should be the true definition of insanity, in my opinion.

Take the lead and be a leader by purging anything, or anyone for that matter, if it doesn't align with your destiny or goals.

GET OUT OF YOUR FEELINGS. GET THE JOB DONE

At times, your feelings will deceive you. They will lead you astray and make you believe that something is the truth, when in reality, it's the complete opposite. If you're not careful, you can miss out on major things that are supposed to happen to and for you. This world is filled with so many distractions.

Nowadays, we are so moved by situations, deaths, sicknesses and natural disasters, and yet when a celebrity wears a fancy expensive gown on the red carpet our attention is immediately taken away from the bigger issues.

Moreover, the media is such a powerful entity. It influences millions of people all at one time. It has the ability to convince you of the clothes you should wear and the food you should eat, it can instill fear in your heart, and it could transition your positive thinking to negative, in an instant.

The media can easily distort your image of the world from being a peaceful and loving place to a fearful place, by exposing you to the deadly occurrences that are happening in third world countries. It's amazing how something so simple can have such an influence on your day.

Don't get me wrong, I have nothing against the media. A great piece of my career was working for a news station as a reporter, so the media industry has my total and sincerest respect. My only point for mentioning the media was to make you aware of how distractions can happen.

See, even this is an example in itself. You've been distracted this whole time by my referencing the media and have missed, or forgotten, my initial statement. It's all tied together.

Going back to my main point, when we are distracted by our feelings, we can quickly miss what's being set up to assist us in accomplishing our goals. How many times have we allowed our feelings to steer us from the clear path to victory?

These disloyal subjects (feelings) have deceived us for far too long. How many times have we lusted after a person and mistaken it for love? How many times have we fooled ourselves into believing something was for us and years later wondered, *What was I thinking?*

You were simply being led by your emotions and feelings, instead of discerning what was important for you at the time.

Touché.

I've been there as well. As a matter of fact, I'm currently there, as we speak. I've been single for some time now. I know, I know. Someone would ask, "Why is someone as beautiful and amazing as you are single?"

I love when this question comes around. It's simple. I'm single because this book isn't finished yet. Do I want a committed relationship? Of course. But, I had to consider that in this season of my life, regardless of what my heart currently wants, a relationship would be a distraction. I gave up something, which I wanted but deemed a distraction in this season, in order to reach my goal.

Finishing this book is my primary focus. I don't know about anyone else, but I pour my entire self into everything that I do. So, at this time I had to delay my gratification to accomplish my goal of finishing this book.

Whether you're single or in a committed relationship, you're attempting to manage your feelings all while trying to commit 100% to fulfilling your dreams. Doesn't that sound pretty challenging?

Let me help. In this very moment, you have to be so sharp and keen on the vision, that nothing and no one can get in the way of finishing.

The challenge that was sent to assist me with finishing this book came in the form of a man. Not any ordinary man, but a fine man! On top of that, he was everything I've ever asked and prayed for.

It's funny because when I think about it, I thought this was God playing a trick on me. Like, really God? Why would you send my help in this form? You could've sent a nice lady in her mid '60s, who once worked as a librarian. However, that wouldn't have been as effective. We needed content for this chapter, so I welcomed the challenge.

Timing is everything. Everything that is supposed to happen in your life, will. You have to trust that all the pieces will align exactly how they should.

In an instant, I had to cut the distraction of focusing on my attraction to him and rely solely on the bigger picture. This dream is bigger than me; it will bless everyone around me, as well as the person reading this book.

It was created with you in mind, so I'm thankful that I was chosen to go through tough decision-making in order for you not to have to go down the same road as I did. I took the lesson and acknowledged that being attracted to this fine chocolate brother was simply a distraction for this time.

That doesn't diminish his value as an amazing person, however, my "A game" had to be on point and I had to cut every distraction in my way. When the time is right, everything that is supposed to happen will happen.

I realized that I couldn't afford to attach my feelings to a situation that would have thrown me off from accomplishing the assignment. At the time, I wasn't as emotionally stable to balance falling for him and finishing this book. I had to choose one. I was being tested.

I had to finally show that I wasn't willing to throw everything away that I wanted for some "eye candy." I simply wasn't ready, and needed to refocus. This is me accepting my truth. I hope you will do the same.

An article in the online version of *Psychology Today* referenced feelings as "an emotional experience that is brief and episodic."

Brief, meaning it's fleeting, temporary and will quickly end. Episodic, meaning there will be occasional periods when your feelings will try to take over. They will grab a hold of your imagination and allow you to believe that what you are currently feeling will be a forever situation. How many times have we experienced this?

Instead of taking full accountability and dismissing the fleeting feeling that comes with the territory, leave your feelings behind and flourish.

LEAVE LASTING IMPRESSIONS

News flash! Not everyone will like you. It's almost inevitable. However, there will be so many other people out there who will love and adore you. They will forever be with you along your life journey and will love you unconditionally.

Take this nugget with you: Leaving lasting impressions will always put you in front of the right people. People will remember you for how you made them feel. It is your duty to leave people with a sweet taste of that amazing personality of yours.

This has to be intentional. Even if things didn't work out with a friendship or relationship, that person should leave the situation knowing that you were a great person to them regardless of how things ended between you two.

Make people remember you. I vowed that I would never leave someone wanting to say that I wronged them intentionally. I'm a conflict resolution specialist. If I need to end a situation I will do so, but on the terms that it ends peacefully.

I'm not responsible for how you treat me, however, I'm held accountable for the way I react toward you. It may be tough to handle ending things this way, but it will leave a lasting impression if you handle the situation in a better fashion, instead of the typical kicking, fighting and screaming.

YOUR CHARACTER IS PRIORITY

"The true test of a man's character is what he does when no one else is watching."

—John Wooden

Your character is your identity. The way you treat people and react when things aren't going exactly the way you planned shows who you really are as a person. If you were to leave this earth today, what would people say about you?

Were you loving, thoughtful, and kind-hearted? Or were you hateful, jealous, mean and conniving? Your character is a main part of who you are. With that being said, how will you now take this very second to make positive changes to your identity?

You can't let people take you out of your character. When I worked in the high-end luxury industry, I was often selected to attend different events and trips to interact with high-end and high-roller clients that some of my counterparts weren't selected to attend.

The counterparts I'm referencing were dedicated to being number one in the industry and were determined, by any means, to get to the top. You wouldn't believe me if I told you some of the things they did to secure first place.

However, I was chosen to represent my company. Why was I chosen to attend? It wasn't that I was better than anyone; it wasn't that I was nicer, kinder or prettier. I wasn't the top sales person, nor did I reach my quotas every month. It was simple.

My character superseded my talent. I did a splendid job at that. I am not saying this to brag about the accolades that I've received. But what I am saying is, when people can trust your decision-making and ethical values, they will choose you every time.

You aren't a liability to them. You will be accountable, and they are certain that you're living up to the standards that the company holds you to.

Some people believe that because they work extremely hard and bring in tons of profit, that it is enough. Wrong. If you believe that to be true, you might as well forget about it, because those talents and skills will only take you so far. You may be able to get into the door, but how you plan on staying in that door is the real question.

Dreamers Action Challenge #5:

This challenge consists of taking an assessment that will "test" your character. There are no right or wrong answers. The purpose of the test is to increase your awareness of how to handle situations, all the while, checking your character. It's time to face the facts and address your character, whether positive or negative, head on. Select an answer and write them down in your journaling notebook.

What you will need:
- A pen
- Your journaling notebook
- About 5–10 minutes

What you will do:
1. In a situation where someone does something that completely rubs you the wrong way, how should you react?

    a. Immediately get upset and tell the person off before even getting all of the facts to the situation.

    b. Take a deep breath, count to 10 and then come back in 24 hours once you've had time to evaluate the situation and address it.

    c. Stay completely quiet while the person hurls insults and rude remarks at you.

2. What do you do if a person is being condescending and belittling someone else when you're around?

a. Make the person aware that their attitude wasn't appropriate and suggest other ways they could've spoken to the person.

b. Walk away as if you didn't hear the interaction.

c. If there is a higher authority around, make them aware of the situation.

Note: Review your answers. How do your responses make you feel? Ask a friend to review your answers and give you feedback on what they think is the right way to handle situations like this. Together, work on ways to improve your character, if necessary. Start making more positive judgments and make improvements toward a healthier character.

STEP FIVE

DREAMERS HUSTLE

"Things come to those who wait, but only the things left by those who hustle."

—Abraham Lincoln

Developing a "hustler's mentality" can work to your advantage. Now, I'm not speaking of the negative connotation of the word that many may consider when they hear the word "hustler." But here's a reality check: Nothing will be given to you.

No one owes you anything, not even the parents who brought you into this world. Once you've accepted that, this journey can become remarkably easier. Put in the work for yourself. Cut your pity party and get out there and do something. Do you want more money? Then find a better job or start a business that will pay you what you're worth.

Work that vision that's been driving you crazy to start. This may sound harsh, but the reality is if you want more, you have to do more. You have to do the work. I can be the first to say your potential is beyond anything that I've ever seen.

But, if you aren't tapping into your potential, it will all mean absolutely nothing. You may have to find a side hustle until you can afford to have the lifestyle you want.

You may have to temporarily work a 9 to 5 to support your actionable dreams. Be a waitress at a high-end restaurant, a chef, anything that can put extra change into your pockets. Or, if working for someone doesn't work for you, use your gifts to create your own financial stability.

For example, while in college, a colleague and I started a clothing boutique that catered to unique women who loved unique fashion. We used our financial aid reimbursement and invested in our idea.

Initially it didn't grow to a rapid success. But the fact that we planned and had a vision for another stream of revenue worked in our favor. It was all about taking the initiative to change our circumstances. It was important that we created our reality and didn't complain about what we didn't have. We realized, ultimately, that we could create our own destiny, so we went for it.

WHAT'S YOUR DEFINITION OF A HUSTLER?

*"I see myself as a natural born hustler, a true hustler,
in every sense of the word. I took nothin', I took
the opportunities, I worked at the most menial and
degrading job and built myself up so I could get it to
where I owned it. I went from having somebody manage
me to me hiring the person that works my management
company. I changed everything. I realized my destiny
in a matter of five years, you know what I'm saying. I
made myself a millionaire. I made millions for a lot of
people, now it's time to make millions for myself, you
know what I'm saying. I made millions for the record
companies, I made millions for these movie companies,
now I'm gonna millions for us."*

—Tupac

Hustling means never taking "no" for an answer and going the extra mile to get what you want and get noticed. So many people have told me that they are tired of their financial situation.

They are burdened in debt and wish they could have more. My number one question to them every time is, "What are YOU doing to change your situation?" I have no right to complain about where I am in life if I'm not taking the necessary action to change my current status. I know you've heard this before, "I'm praying for a change and just waiting on God, but I'm still in the same place."

First of all, stop blaming God and start taking accountability for where you are in your life. Get up off your complaints and find something that can bring a whirlwind of change for you. Set yourself up for your family, friends and unborn children.

Now, I'm not saying not to pray and ask for guidance, understanding, resources and strength to fulfill the task, but you can't just ask God to give you something that you barely put in any time or effort to obtain.

We were created to work. It's in our DNA to subdue, make fruitful, replenish and dominate this earth. This is my interpretation of the scripture I quoted earlier in the book (Genesis 1:28).

In no way, shape or form am I saying this is easy. If anything, I'm telling you that this will be, at times, a strenuous task. It will challenge you but ultimately make you better. There should be no shame in working several legal jobs to create more wealth for yourself.

Not every one has the opportunity to make it to college and come out with a job paying six figures. Your story has been written a little differently. That doesn't make you any less of a person. But you have the power to make it happen. You have the ability to create whatever you want.

That leads me to my next point. Seriously, if you want something as bad as you want to breathe, you'll do what it takes to get it.

I remember when I first moved, I encountered a young

man who was 20-years-old. He had the dream job that I always wanted, or, thought I wanted. He worked in the media department for a well-known NFL organization. I had to ask him, "How in the world did you get this job? What did you do that I didn't?"

To my surprise, his strategy was a bit different from the traditional online application submission. He explained how he printed out 200 copies of his resume and personalized his cover letter to address each director of the different departments where he was seeking employment.

After he packaged all 200, he overnighted each one, requiring a signature of the individual it was addressed to, to assure they received it. Out of the 200 submissions, he received four call backs, and from that point, he had viable options to choose from.

Now, that's what I call a "hustler." He wasn't going to take "no" for an answer, and he didn't do what the average "Joe Schmo" did when it came to getting what he wanted. It was the little details that others weren't doing that made him stand out. He went the extra mile and received better results.

DON'T KNOCK ON THE DOOR. KICK IT DOWN

"No" doesn't exist—not when it comes to your dreams, at least. You can find any loophole to getting what you need. You can have every single thing you want. Be clear and precise. Write everything down to the very last detail.

(If you need help with this, refer back to the Dreamers Think BIG! chapter). Don't miss a beat.

I'm telling you that NOTHING comes to a sleeper but a dream. If there is something that you desire to change with total conviction, change it. This world is so massive; it's an entire universe full of different people, personalities, religions, cultures, beliefs and many other things.

We have to develop the attitude of fearlessness and bravery, while embracing the mentality of kicking down the door of opportunity at the same time. Currently, I am listening to Myleik Teele, owner of CurlBox. On an episode on her #MyTaughtYou podcast, she is speaking with Datwon Thomas, editor-in-chief of VIBE magazine.

He literally spoke about pursuing your dreams with "reckless abandon." According to Merriam-Webster's online dictionary, the term "reckless abandon" means to *do something in a very wild way*. Use this concept to chase every single dream with reckless abandon, without regard for the unknown.

Raise your hand if you feel that you deserve to sit still, as everyone and everything progresses and passes you by? I didn't think you would want that. You have the ability to acquire and retain all necessary knowledge, wisdom and insight to go after the things that you've dreamt about. By all means, you deserve to have it if you will chase that opportunity like it's the last thing left on this earth.

I've had people tell me, "I'll wait for it to happen. I know this opportunity is here, but I'm just waiting." As everything around them is changing and growing, they are still waiting—spiritually disconnected and asleep on what's right in front of them.

If I put $1,000,000,000 in front of you and said all you have to do is get up, take it, and it's yours, would you still sit down, second-guessing if this is your reality? Would you wonder whether this were real? Would you tell me, "I'll wait to see if this is going to happen?" Or, would you get up and grab what is available to you?

Making excuses and procrastinating should've been added to the seven deadly sins. There are some people who are waiting and watching, hoping and praying that they will get this information. But they still won't move. We have to become sensitive to the atmosphere around us.

I've been attacked mentally and emotionally when it comes to helping others. The very thing that I love to do has reversed on me and stabbed me in the back several times. I used to pray and ask God, "Why would you give me such a huge heart to help others and every time I turn around I am being attacked by people?"

The more I tried to help, the more opposition I received. Some people who I have known since I was a kid playing on the playground have betrayed me. They told me that I thought I was too good for them and that I have changed.

It felt as if the ones who I loved the most would find ways to continually throw me under the bus. Did that change my perspective on helping, reaching and teaching?

Absolutely not.

It fueled me. I wanted to continue to push forward, whether I had their support or not, and I would love them from a distance, while wishing them nothing but the best. It still hurt deeply. I felt saddened, emotional and upset, but I wasn't going to let anything or anyone stand in my way. I was going to prove that I could live my life with purpose. I wasn't going to be afraid.

I plan on continuing to push myself into this journey until I have no more to give. Connecting with myself and collaborating with God makes the possibilities endless.

Dreamers Action Challenge #6:

This challenge will increase your positive energy and will be a daily reminder of how great you are.

What you will need:
- Your journaling notebook
- A pen

What you will do:
On one sheet of paper write down 10 words that describe a positive aspect of your character, what you represent or what you have a love for. (Some words I came up with for myself are love, peace, joy, respect, generosity, etc.).

After writing down the words, sit quietly for 10 minutes.

Meditate silently. Replay the 10 words in your head and what they look like for you. (When I thought of the word generosity it reminded me that I feel joy in my heart when I give to others).

Allow yourself to feel positivity, and increase your awareness within yourself.

Repeat this exercise whenever you don't feel your best. Allow yourself to feel and embrace your higher inner self.

STEP SIX

DREAMERS MAXIMIZE

One thing I know about every dreamer is that they are ambitious and are go-getters. They aren't slouchy, lazy or stagnant. They will literally show you how to make a dollar out of fifteen cents.

However, they wouldn't be able to do all of these things alone. In fact, they have an entire team behind them to assist with making it happen—a team that equips them with all they need. Dreamers can then go forth and do all the things they need to do to increase their wealth.

I remember reading about the founder of Chick-fil-A, S. Truett Cathy, where he shared a major principle that has been the cornerstone of the company's success.

Here's the story from Jimmylarche.com:

Several years ago the executive leadership team of Chick-fil-a had worked for quite some time on how to keep up with the competitive challenge created in their industry by Boston Chicken (later known as *Boston Market*). After a period of intense research and market studies, a group of young visionary leaders with big ideas and bright strategies found themselves in a committee room of frenzied debate over how to get *bigger* faster!

At the height of the dialogue, Truett Cathy, the founder of Chick-fil-a began to pound on the table, which was very uncharacteristic of this admirable leader. When every eye in the room turned to him, he exclaimed that he was sick and tired of all this talk about getting *bigger*. Then he said, "If we get better our customers will demand we get bigger!"

Over years of competing in the volatile food service industry, Cathy knew the secret to success and its significance. It was getting better before you get bigger.

This was such a pivotal moment of success for me. Instead of trying to get more people to follow my vision, it made sense to produce better content—better videos, better graphics, better effects, better lighting. Quality content is truly king. It was time to get better with my product and implement "must have" solutions. It was time to improve the technical aspects and everything that I had learned.

Darren Hardy, a well-known motivational speaker, spoke on the topic "Secrets of Great Achievers" and said, "Do fewer things, more often, and get better at them. Learn how to take your efforts to the next level by focusing on the top three things and doing nothing else but that. Learn the power of saying 'no,' while you give unprecedented focus to your top three priorities."

He also mentioned, "We are addicted to distractions. We yearn for them. It's a justifiable excuse to be distracted." This statement couldn't be anything less than the truth. Use this time to grow, maximize and limit all distractions. It's time to produce great work. Do that by creating an environment that requires you to focus.

Create such an intense place of focus that nothing or nobody else matters. All that matters is that you finalize your plans. All that matters is that you produce excellent work.

THE IMPORTANCE OF SOCIAL CAPITAL

Who do you know? Who can help you get to the next level? Who can you reach out to if you need a favor? What relationships have you built just in case you need advice?

Who could you call if you need a helping hand? Where have you sowed seeds by helping others, just in case you need help one day? If you can't answer any of these questions I recommend that you drop what you're doing and start relationship-building now.

According to Dictionary.com, social capital is "The network of social connections that exists between people and their shared values and norms of behavior, which enable and encourage mutually advantageous social cooperation."

It is built on establishing trust in your networks. Social

capital is considered the new relationship currency. It's a wealthy place to be, especially when you have people you can refer to if you need advice or insight. What type of world would we live in if we had no one to call for help?

One thing I always remember my mother saying to me is, "People need people." You simply can't survive without the love and help of others. It goes back to the willingness to be attentive to others and serve them first.

Have you considered what the term "serving" actually means? It's when you can selflessly give to another person without expecting anything in return. We have to learn to give ourselves, our time and assistance to others. We live in a generation that has the mentality of what have you done for me lately?

But when you can truly give to someone and help them without expecting something in return, you're putting out that same intentional energy that will circle back around to you.

I recently finished a photo shoot which I originally thought I would use for this book. When my pictures came back, they weren't exactly how I wanted them to be edited. The first thought that came across my mind was, *Who can I call to help me?*

I needed the pictures to be perfect and exactly how I wanted them to look. I reached out to a photographer I knew and asked if he could assist. Despite the fact that we haven't spoken in a while, he assisted me with his expertise, and the pictures came out exceptionally well. What if I hadn't built that bridge of trust with the photographer?

What if I had ruined our relationship by not doing "good business" with him in the past? What if I didn't make time to connect with this photographer from time to time? What if I was so consumed in myself, that I forgot who helped me when I needed it the most?

I have remained connected to the relationships I've built over the years. To add pleasure to principle, I've sowed seeds along the way. I've done work for free. I've helped people who couldn't pay me with anything except a smile.

I've done projects and spoken to students without expecting a dollar in return. Why? Well, I understand the principle of sowing. I believe that whatever you put out there will come back to you hundredfold. Now, I'm not telling you to go out there and give your talent and skills away for free every time.

But, what I am saying, is to sow seeds of love, kindness and time. It's not always about a dollar. Most importantly, because I gave of myself in that way, whenever I needed a favor or for someone to come through for me, they typically did it without question.

My first job working at a local station was referred to me by someone I knew. It was from the connection and relationship I built with that person in college.

Every place I've been, or every job I've received, was

because of a relationship I've built with another person. Build your bank account full of relationship currency and watch your entire life triple in funds.

YOUR NETWORK IS YOUR NET WORTH

Whomever you have in your immediate circle is equal to the amount of revenue you have coming in. I know you've heard the sayings, "If you're the smartest person in the room then you're in the wrong room," or "Show me your friends and I'll tell you who you are."

The people around you should increase you, expand you, challenge you, motivate you and, most important, teach you how to bring revenue into your life. If the people around you make you feel drained or are always complaining about what they don't have, then there's something you need to do immediately. You need to remove yourself from that circle as soon as possible. You can truly love people from a distance.

There's a world out there that you haven't even seen yet. But you may not see it if you remain in the same comfortable circle that isn't elevating you. Writer and speaker, Porter Gale, wrote an article for the *Huffington Post* titled "Why Your Network Is Your Net Worth." The article said, "I believe your social capital, or your ability to build a network of authentic personal and professional relationships, not your financial capital, is the most important asset in your portfolio."

My calm, objective opinion is to take some time today to

check your circle.

UTILIZE YOUR CONNECTIONS

You didn't go about sowing seeds, doing free work and sacrificing long days and time just for nothing. Now, I'm not saying do for others out of the expectation that they will do something for you one day. No, do it wholeheartedly with no ulterior motive.

However, don't believe for a second that you will not be rewarded for being an answer. Those honest and genuine relationships that you've built, utilize them. If you need an answer, reach back to a mentor. If you need legal advice, reach back to the attorney that you did work for.

If you need a connection, call the videographer who wouldn't mind helping you out because he remembered when you toted his equipment up the highest of seven hills for him (Florida A&M University pun intended). Utilize these nurtured relationships to get to the next level.

If you've genuinely helped people and did it with a pure heart, I know they wouldn't mind reaching back out to help you. Your sacrifice and work will never be in vain if you help others. A pure heart can take you a lot farther than being conniving and deceitful.

If you plan to take it up a notch, humble yourself and reach back for help. There's nothing wrong with not having all the answers. But, the smartest, most logical thing to do is to get help and get it fast. You're full of resources and connections; you just haven't taken the time to realize it. Save yourself the headache and money by not going to your local expert, but reaping the benefits from the relationships you've already built.

SOCIAL NETWORKS HAVE VALUE

Social media outlets can impact millions of users at one click of a button. The question isn't *if* social media is impactful; we already know that answer. The real question here is, why aren't we using it to impact the lives of millions?

Instead of taking our next best selfie or the famous mirror pic to upload on our pages, why don't we try to post something meaningful and insightful?

I remember when I was in junior high, there was a security guard whom everyone knew. He was so down to earth and well respected. One day I got into some trouble at school and was nearly suspended, which wasn't good news, especially if my parents were going to find out.

I would've been grounded for months and could've kissed the quickly approaching homecoming dance goodbye. He said something so mind-blowing to me that until this day, I still remember it. He said, "No matter where you are, someone is always watching you. We may think we are getting away with something, but it always has its way of coming back around to either haunt us or reward us." He was absolutely right.

That goes back to my main point. Someone is always watching your social media page. Even if they aren't commenting or liking your pictures, they are watching. They are scrolling up and down your feed hoping and praying that they don't accidently "double tap."

If you see someone posting alcohol, late-night party outings and pictures of them passed out all of the time, what would be your perception of that person? Exactly. It's the same for all of us who use it. Instead of venting about how horrible life is, and why we can't find a good, stable relationship, why don't we use it to better ourselves and the people around us?

We never know how we can impact others. Maybe our inspirational posts may prevent someone from committing suicide. Not to mention, some job applications now require a social media background check. If the hiring boss wants to know anything about you, all they need to do is look up your social media handle and scan away.

People will ask for your social media handle before your business cards nowadays. You are what you post, so post wisely.

Dreamers Action Challenge #7:

This challenge will assist you in realizing who is a part of your social network and how they can assist you with being your best self.

What you will need:
- Your journaling notebook
- A pen

What you will do:
Draw three sections on a page in your journal. In the first section you will list five people who are in your social network. These are the people who can help you get to the next level in your business or business ideas. They can be family, friends and mentors. The next section will be titled, "What can I do to help this person with something?" The last section will be, "What can I learn from this person to be the best version of myself?" Answer the questions for each person you've selected.

Reach out to these five people and offer your help. Also, ask if they would have time to assist you with the things you've written in the last section. This will help you grow in the areas where you need assistance and build a strong, connected social network.

STEP SEVEN

DREAMING IN THE "I AM"

My entire perspective has changed ever since I learned to speak using the power of "I AM." It's like I've been introduced to a new part of the English language that I wasn't taught in school. I've had to reconstruct my thoughts to align with my words, and from this, my actions have had successful results. This wasn't an easy process.

I used to think very negatively. I used to believe that I wasn't worthy of having a great life and that I wasn't enough. I was just living. If things didn't work out, my first thought would be, *It just wasn't for me.* What if I had the power to change what I was thinking so it could create the reality that I wanted to live in? I found my power with a really simple formula.

The power of using "I AM" goes back to a scripture in my favorite book. The reference is from Exodus 3 (NIV). Moses was out tending to the flock when the Angel of the Lord appeared from within a bush. Moses saw that the bush was on fire, but it did not burn up. As he drew closer, God called him from within the bush and began to speak to him. As we move further along the story, the Lord saw the misery of his people in Egypt—the Israelites were at the mercy of the Egyptians. God saw their suffering and wanted to free them from the oppression they were facing.

I could imagine the expression of total shock on Moses's face when he realized that God had chosen him to go to Pharaoh to bring the Israelites out of Egypt. Moses asked, "Who am I that I should go to Pharaoh to bring the Israelites out of Egypt?" God reassured him that he would be with him the whole way, so he shouldn't fear.

But Moses didn't feel qualified. The interesting part is, he was absolutely right. He wasn't qualified. A wise man once told me, "God doesn't call the qualified; He qualifies the called." You don't have to have all the training, degrees or certifications; all you need is a small mustard seed of faith.

The dialogue here then becomes quite interesting. Moses says, "Suppose I go to the Israelites and say to them, 'The God of your fathers has sent me to you.' And they ask me, 'What is his name?' Then what shall I tell them?"

There is so much intensity now, because Moses doesn't feel ready or even prepared to take on such a task. The story continues as God says to Moses, "I AM who I AM. This is what you are to say to the Israelites: 'I AM has sent me to you.'"

When I think of that subtle but quite powerful statement, it allows me to see the significance of the "I AM." Whatever we connect to the words I AM—in the name of God—will manifest on this earth for us.

So, if we say and believe that "I AM successful, I AM powerful, I AM healed, I AM worthy, I AM loved and I AM qualified," the very words that we connect to "I AM" will happen for us. Start speaking positivity into your environment and start feeling the emotion behind what you're speaking.

Words are so powerful; now imagine adding God into the equation. You've just created an avalanche of miracles coming your way.

There's a powerful exchange that happens to you and the atmosphere when you open your mouth and proudly declare something. It makes you feel powerful, qualified and ready to conquer whatever it is that you want to see happen for yourself.

However, this task is quite challenging. Honestly, I've been on this journey of transitioning my thoughts, words and actions for the past year, and I truly can tell the difference.

It feels like a new life change is happening in and through me. It's as if I am reprogramming what I've learned about the English language and am implementing new verbiage to speak.

Instead of feeling less than, disqualified and pessimistic,

I am changing what I say to create a better world for me to live in. Often times, we underestimate the fact that thoughts and words hold so much power.

Your thoughts can make you feel happy, respected, loved and kind. They also have the power to cause illness in the body, or make you feel sad, upset and angry. We have the power with our words to change our circumstance.

With this newfound way of thinking and speaking, I can confidently say my entire life has changed. The outcome of my situations have become more positive, which has resulted in a more positive lifestyle. I deliberately practiced thinking my way into new opportunities and the lifestyles that I wanted. Why didn't I understand this concept much earlier?

If I had known then what I know now, I could've been further along in life. But that's irrelevant at this point. The important thing is to move forward today.

I've created a formula that will assist you in grasping this concept a lot easier than I did. Hey, I am here for you! We are in this thing together. We will conquer this and spread it to the masses. Here's the formula:

Your thoughts + Your words + Your actions = Your reality.

Pretty simple right? Pat yourself on the back because you're almost on your way to freeing your mind, body and spirit.

Let's say for instance, you want to start a business, but

have no clue where to start. You're on the right track because you've put thought into creating something that you want.

Next would be to start speaking it into existence. "I AM a successful business owner, I AM running a Fortune 500 hundred company, I AM bringing value to my clients through my creative products."

Lastly, put action on what it is you want. One of the most important keys to this process is to put your wheels in motion. You'll start off not knowing where the resources, funding or people are, but make sure you simply just apply action.

Unfortunately, as you begin this process, a slew of negative thoughts will start to ring loudly and disturbingly in your mind. The key is to stop those negative thoughts in their tracks.

Don't allow self-doubt to corrupt your inner being and your creative ideas with thoughts like:

> *You aren't qualified!*
> *You're surrounded in debt; how will you start a business?*
> *You haven't been trained in this field!*
> *How do you expect to win when there are millions of people out there smarter than you?*

Use those thoughts as motivation to start thinking positively and start decreeing your positive "I AM" affirmations today. Affirmations like:

I AM going to make a difference!
I AM going to have a successful and influential business.
I AM going to change the world with my creative idea.
I AM going to reach others who need the assistance from my business.
I AM worthy to grow a successful network!
I AM attracting the right resources I need now!

If you can start to think more positive thoughts about yourself and about the environment around you, you'll start to see a drastic positive change occur.

This change will nurture the right mindset and allow opportunities and connections to flow into your life. You'll become more motivated to stay on the path of creating a better life for yourself.

All of this comes from my organization, The I AM Community. We are a community of dreamers who encourage self-love and self-awareness through "I AM" affirmations. We believe that if you think something, say it and put action toward it, it can become your reality.

Our message and results are so strong that we have taken our mission to all social media outlets to spread the good news of the power of "I AM" affirmations.

This journey started with a challenge that I took to social media. I remember struggling with low self-esteem and self-confidence. I didn't really believe in myself as people thought I did, so I figured I needed to have a vulnerable moment with myself and with others.

I wrote a long page of positive "I AM" affirmations, such as "I AM worthy of love. I AM going to be a loving wife one day. I AM creative, I AM intelligent, I AM going to inspire and impact this generation." I then posted it on my personal Instagram page, with a caption and hashtag: the #IAMChallenge.

This was extremely new to me; I was open, yet at peace with my decision to share, with hopes that it would inspire others. The challenge spread like wildfire to my network of followers, and upon posting I realized the hashtag already had momentum from previous I AM challenges.

I then realized that what was started was a movement and much more than a hashtag. It was truly a community of people who believed in the same things. We felt that affirming ourselves and thinking positively could change our circumstance. More importantly, we could encourage each other through the process.

These two words, "I AM," address something far beyond what the eyes can see. They speak to one special place that many people are afraid to visit and discuss: the "V" word. Before your mind starts to wander off, let me explain.

VULNERABILITY

Through social media, we have opened ourselves up to share our deepest thoughts and desires on a public platform of who we believe we are. It is indeed a commendable act. It took some time, but I no longer believe in fear. This is something I will touch on in-depth later in this chapter.

I used to be so afraid to open up to people and share my deepest thoughts about myself. I've never dealt well with rejection. In fact, I still struggle with it from time to time, but I am learning to allow this fleeting objection to pass on by like every other negative emotion that I may have faced.

I remember when being open was a breeze for me, especially in relationships. I will never forget what it was like to date a guy for more than three years who rarely showed emotion or verbally expressed his love for me. He was so guarded. In turn, it made me the same way. Trying to get him to say nice things was like pulling teeth.

When I would get upset about something between us and cry about it, instead of consoling me, he would make me feel like crying about it was a waste of time. Instead of drawing nearer, it pushed me away and made me into a cold person toward him. I was full of bitterness and the fear of rejection. I believed that my thoughts and feelings were minuscule and unimportant.

Fortunately, that situation has not defined me. Now that I have healed, I realize that my thoughts, ideas, emotions and my very being are far too important not to acknowledge. I AM more than enough. I matter, and it is alright to be open and vulnerable. In this day and age, vulnerability is seen as a weak trait. People are afraid to be their authentic selves out of the fear of being ridiculed and teased. Vulnerability can be one of the most beautiful feelings, if you allow it to be. Now, in no way shape or form am I advising you to run out there and be free and open with every person you encounter.

That would be a little ridiculous. What I am saying is, be discerning as to the right people to open up with.

We can be so closed off and afraid to love because of what someone else has done to us, or because we fear the other person won't feel the same way.

We create these walls as a defense mechanism to block away anything that even looked like it had intent to hurt us. We keep everyone at arm's length, hoping they won't attempt to tear down the barriers we've built up.

In turn, we can't give or receive love, joy, courage, gratitude and peace. We are so cold and distant that our hearts have built their own personal iceboxes. (Cue Omarion's song "Ice Box").

The worst part is the negative thoughts associated with the walls we've built up. We now believe that no one loves us, something is wrong with us and that we will never find true love. We repeat these lies in our minds as if we were chanting the "Om" mantra during meditation.

We search, attempting to find out why this happened to us. Why have we experienced so much pain? When did we become so closed off and locked away? People are afraid of being their authentic selves out of the fear of things not working out. We blame ourselves for people not loving us the way we thought we should have been loved.

That one experience with rejection has brought us to a spiral of self-hate and self-pity. See how this works? From one situation of being rejected, we now choose to blame ourselves for all that has happened to us.

Hey, someone has to take the blame, right? It is easy to forgive someone else instead of ourselves. So we beat ourselves up, not realizing that we are creating an atmosphere of self-defeat.

Close your eyes and imagine a person you truly admire. To you, this person is perfect in his/her own right. In your mind, they can do no wrong. But let's say one day this perfect person went to the grocery store and stole something.

Would you forgive them? Would you believe that they just had a weak moment and could get through this? If the answer is yes, then you have to ask yourself a few things:

If you can give someone that benefit of the doubt, why can't you do that for yourself? Why can't you forgive yourself for your shortcomings and understand that everything in life is a teachable moment?

Past mistakes were meant to build us up in strength and stature and allow us to strive for healthy personal growth. The symptoms of the lack of vulnerability and the lack of self-forgiveness can be treated, once exposed. You must start with the first step: loving yourself. You matter and are more than enough. If you are still here on this big, green earth, then you still have purpose.

You're not done yet. Love yourself and be certain that there is no one else on this earth that can do it like you do. From your fingerprints, to the pace of your heartbeat, you are like no other in this world.

Even if you have a twin sister or brother, you are unique. You were carefully created and sought after; precious time was spent creating you. You were thought about enough down to the womb you grew in. The strategy behind your development is beyond anything the human mind can fathom.

You're unique and special and created with care. No matter what this life has or will bring, you deserve all of the good things that it has to offer. Though I may not know you personally, I genuinely believe and know this to be true. "Love yourself" is something many people preach to do, but never exactly say how to do it. So let me explain. The first step to loving yourself is accepting who you are, flaws and all.

Embrace every single little quirky detail about yourself. Love and appreciate your personality. If you have a bad habit that you absolutely can't stand, accept it. Be gentle with yourself to allow yourself the time to grow through that habit until it isn't a part of who you are any longer. If you think there are others who are smarter or more qualified at something than you are, accept it. Don't beat yourself up.

As author Don Miguel Ruiz wrote in his book The Four Agreements, you should "always do your best." As long as you know you've put forth your best effort to achieve something that's all anyone can truly ask for. Accept yourself for all that you are. Value your creativity and all that you have. Where you are in life is exactly where you should be, but always take the proper measures to grow and challenge yourself.

Stop what you're doing right now! Drop everything and give yourself a great big bear hug. You deserve it. Self-love is truly the best love. You can't depend on anyone to love you like you can love yourself.

The next step is to stop trying to prove yourself to others. People will see your worth once you've realized it yourself. You don't have to prove anything. People will naturally connect with the confidence you have and want more of it.

From here on out, focus every single moment on speaking the right "I AM," and connect to being vulnerable. Whatever follows "I AM," you will become. The wrong "I AM" can keep you from having all that you should and could have. If you want to see something change, start proclaiming your positive "I AM" affirmations and start reaching for the finish line.

"I AM" VULNERABLE

Vulnerability is such a huge concept that I am going to take a few more paragraphs to expound on it. Have you ever been at the place where you wanted to express yourself but you didn't understand how, exactly, to do it?

You really wanted to say what you felt deep down in your heart, but because of past experiences you didn't say a word? Have you ever been wounded badly by giving your all in hopes that something special and real would come from it?

It's like you wanted to say something, but you were so scared of the rejection that could possibly come from it? It's such a real place to be in, mentally. When I would date after my previous relationship, I had a huge wall built.

Seriously, if I loved you or even liked you I would never express it. I was so afraid to be rejected and wounded again, so I went along being closed off and scared like a small child. It was indeed a challenge that I had to face if I wanted to love or be loved again. I had to swallow my pride and understand that this current situation wasn't that past experience.

We are so much more powerful than we think. We can control the atmosphere of any room that we walk into, just by our very presence. We have the power in the stride of our step and the confidence that exudes from our very being.

When you can't control a situation, that's where trust comes into play. We dedicate so much time to building careers and wealth that we forget to go back to our assigned duty. That's to L-O-V-E.

We've been so hurt and wounded by people and situations, that we forget that love can conquer anything. You know what I believe strength is? Strength is loving, trusting and giving, even after you've been wounded.

Shutting down isn't true growth. When we are closed in, we believe that we are safe. If a person can't truly see me for all that I am, then everything will be alright. We tell ourselves, "I shouldn't let anyone in. I'm protecting myself from allowing anyone to hurt me and from feeling the hurt from the past." We walk around not being able to receive love from others because we think we are protecting ourselves.

That is the furthest from the truth. Being closed and locked away from what you think you're protecting yourself from is actually hurting you. I was in this exact mental space some time ago. My ability to be vulnerable was being tested and I didn't even know it.

I was in a position to love on the people who God had blessed me with. Whether that was a family member or friend, I was able to relearn how to be open to give and receive love again, all by being open to vulnerability and acknowledging my own feelings.

Brene Brown, American scholar, author and speaker, did a TED Talk on the power of vulnerability. She has studied vulnerability, courage, worthiness and shame. During her discussion, she expressed why so many people are afraid of vulnerability and what we are actually missing out on when we aren't vulnerable with others.

She talked about an interview she conducted where the people who were comfortable with being vulnerable experienced a sense of worthiness. She stated, "And so these folks had, very simply, the courage to be imperfect. They had the compassion to be kind to themselves first and then to others, because, as it turns out, we can't practice compassion with other people if we can't treat ourselves kindly."

That concept will sound foreign, especially to someone who cringes at the thought of being vulnerable. But, the journey to vulnerability has to begin if you desire to have all that you want and deserve out of this thing called life and let go of who others think you should be.

Vulnerability is important to a dreamer because you're able to be your true self. It is significant for me as a dreamer to be who I truly am so I can relate to others who have been where I've been. I've struggled with being my true self because I was afraid of other people's opinions of me.

I was afraid of being judged and criticized, so I would scale back my vibrant personality so as not to offend others. I now realize that it's totally alright being all that I was created to be. Being vulnerable not only with myself, but with others, has allowed me the chance to learn who I am and accept all of who I was created to be.

I encourage you to do the same. You're great and amazing, and when you're your true, higher self, you can conquer anything.

When we are caught up in being who we aren't, we dim our light. We fall victim to ourselves in order to be liked. Be open and 100% of who you are. If people don't like you for it, that's simply their loss. Be happy and cheerful that you actually know yourself. Love who you genuinely are.

Today, my friends, I share with you a vulnerable, open-to-receive individual who will love anyway, despite the fact of being wounded. I can now look at the past and smile because I know that all the hurt, pain and misfortune prepared me for this moment. My moment. I'm able to love again.

The definition of vulnerability is to be capable of being physically or emotionally wounded. However, let's put a spin on that. Show me that you've been wounded, bruised and mistreated, yet you can still love.

Show me that you can be your higher-self and not respond with your ego. Our reactions and behaviors have been learned, and are not our true selves. With that being said, you can always learn new and better behaviors, or simply start being the best version of yourself.

The act of vulnerability has to start with you. You have to love yourself including your mistakes, flaws and short comings. You have to love yourself beyond your losses.

If you go into any situation that requires you to use your heart, and you're already thinking you'll fail, then that's exactly what will happen. You'll end up possibly jeopardizing the most beautiful blessing that your mind could even fathom because you doubted your ability.

Today, I challenge you to give yourself another shot. I challenge you to be vulnerable.

WHAT DO YOU DESERVE?

When I started being open again, my happiness increased. I had faith and hope again. This ties into dreamers taking action, because I believe when you deal with those small nuances that make you who you are, you'll start finding success in things that you pursue.

When you start understanding who you are and what you deserve you won't compromise for just anything that is handed to you. The wisdom from that understanding tells you who and what to accept, which ultimately creates a standard, which is absolutely necessary.

What are you knowingly accepting that you don't want? What are you settling for because it's convenient and doesn't offer a challenge?

Your standards should dictate the type of friendship, relationship, career—down to the car you'll drive. Your standards are the expectation of how you desire your life to go. You shouldn't lower your standards based on what the majority says, or does.

My mentor told me a story once that really blew my mind. One day after leaving an event, my mentor's fiancée asked their mutual friend if she could give him a lift to his home. The weirdest thing was when he was ready to leave, the woman handed him her keys to her car.

He stood there puzzled, wondering why she would hand the keys to him. Her response was simple, yet powerful: "As a woman, I simply don't drive men around. It's just something that I don't do." He couldn't understand that at first, but it was her standard. He accepted it, and they went on their way.

She could have easily driven him home, but instead, she held steadfast to her standard as a woman who simply doesn't drive men around, even if it's in her car. It may seem different to some, but it's important to develop your standards and stick to them. Never compromise your beliefs—even if it's a bit farfetched to others. You aren't for everybody, and it will show.

BELIEVING BEYOND WHAT YOU CAN SEE

Faith.

When my mom was diagnosed with cancer, it was the hardest thing I'd ever experienced in my life. It pained me to see her pain and realize I was completely incapable of making her feel better.

The one and only thing I could do was pray for her. Each

day, my dependency on myself decreased and merged toward the higher power. When you don't know what to do, when you've cried your last tear, what do you do?

Seriously, if you can answer that question, I would love to hear your insight. Maybe you can possibly help me through this situation. It gets so dark sometimes and life can make you feel so worthless. You know you should be strong, but how do you really do that? What in the world does that actually mean?

What does that look like? Strength? I've tried it and when I couldn't take it any longer on my own, I just believed. I believed that one day, her life would change for the better. I knew that my family's life would change as well. I didn't have much of a choice at this point, right?

I was either going to roll with the punches or fold. Losing had never been in my vocabulary. However, sometimes the strongest people need somebody to lean on, too. What do you do when there is nothing left to do? You stay there, put your shoulders back, hold your head high and stand until certainty appears.

You lean on the embrace and love of the higher power of God. Seriously, what else can you do? When it comes to sickness, there is no one who can change the process of being ill. There is no one who can do anything to change it but God's power. Ultimately, it's his will that will show in the end.

In life, we may not know what the next steps are all the time. We may not know what the next turn is. We may have to take a few wrong turns and detours. But when you start believing beyond what you can actually see, or have faith, it will open up a world of possibility for you.

As a dreamer, you have to have a lot of faith. You have to believe that your plans and goals can be conquered. As a dreamer, you have to stay steadfast in your faith, even when things aren't working in your favor.

I remember there was a time in my life where I felt as if I was getting hit from every direction—everything I was attempting to pursue wasn't working out. I started a women's clothing boutique in college and had to close it four months after being opened.

It hurt so much to lose what I invested time and money into, but I knew I was destined for greatness someway, somehow. I just had to keep pushing through the loss that I'd experienced.

Years later, things started to unfold with my organization, the I AM Community. The number of members that have been a part of this organization and have encouraged one another through this outlet has been remarkable.

The messages and emails that we have received about the organization helping people beat depression and lift themselves out of low self-esteem have showed us that the community was needed and is helping in a positive way.

I have experienced my own personal healing through others sharing their success stories.

The organization has given me a newfound hope that despite what you may have lost, God always has something better waiting for you if you keep moving forward.

Keep your faith. Believe in yourself no matter what happens. Remind yourself that your current situation will not determine your outcome in life. You have what it takes to believe that one day it will come to fruition for you.

I leave you with this: Be the strong dreamer that you were created to be, but promise yourself that you will act today. Chase that dream until it's standing right in front of you.

Keep your focus on finishing all that you start. This journey will get weary. You'll experience sad moments and you will feel like you're doing all of this work for nothing.

However, there is a light at the end of the tunnel if you don't quit. Recite Galatians 6:9 (NIV) whenever you feel like quitting. "Let us not become weary in doing good, for at the proper time we will reap a harvest if we do not give up."

Your answer is deep inside your heart, and no matter how long it takes, finish in excellence. Just as it took me three years to finish this book, with the insight left on these pages you will manifest your dream in a shorter time. Once you reach the goal, pay it forward.

Share your process with someone who may be having a

hard time. Pass the baton and celebrate the person who took off running toward their dreams.

It's time for us. Dreamers, to Take Action!

Dreamers Action Challenge #8:

Write all of your positive "I AM" affirmations on a sheet of paper and recite them every single day. The goal isn't to focus on your current circumstance, but to decree and declare positive "I AM" affirmations into the atmosphere. Whatever you say after "I AM" will come looking for you. That works the same with saying negative "I AM" statements. The goal here is to remain positive.

What you will need:
- A pen
- Your journaling notebook
- Think of the positive "I AM" affirmations you want to use

What you will do:
In order to choose which affirmations to start declaring, we will have to start with a set of questions that will pull from all of your positive traits. Write down and answer these questions:

Who am I?
What am I good at?
What is unique about me?
What sets me apart?
What are my skills?
What are three positive things about me?
What do I love about myself?
What are some of my accomplishments that I am proud of?

Write down all of your positive "I AM" affirmations. These could be affirmations that you already are, or wish to see happen in the near future. Use the answers from your questions above to formulate your affirmations. Here are some examples:

I AM worth it.
I AM more than enough.
I AM focused.
I AM building generational wealth.
I AM successful.

Fill the entire sheet of paper with your beautiful "I AM" affirmations.

Snap a picture of your completed "I AM" affirmation list.

Follow @IAMCommunity_ on Instagram and tag your list. We will gladly repost it.

Post your affirmations in a visible place where you can see them every day.

Recite your "I AM" affirmations with conviction every single day.

Start feeling empowered, enlightened and motivated to go after your dreams.

Visit IAMCommunity.org to view other "I AM" entries and be a part of The I AM Community by getting your very own I AM t-shirt from the website.

You will start to feel empowered, enlightened, loved and reminded to recite your affirmations. You can now wear the shirt that tells everyone about your newfound life.

About The Author

Nikkie Pryce is focused on inspiring and motivating people to put action behind their dreams. Being in the media industry and working directly with the public, she has experience pushing people past their own created limitations. She has earned the title of "self-love influencer" through her organization, The I AM Community.

This social community is comprised of dreamers who encourage self-love and self-awareness, starting with "I AM" affirmations. What all started as a simple journey to finding her own self-love became a phenomenon of connections and solid relationships.

A highly recommended motivational speaker, Nikkie speaks publicly at different events and engagements: corporate conferences, schools, nonprofit organizations, women's retreats, youth girl groups, church functions and many more.

Connect with Nikkie at www.NikkiePryce.com

BOOK NIKKIE TODAY!

Nikkie Pryce's focus is on inspiring and encouraging people to put action behind their dreams. Being in the media industry and working directly with the public, she has the experience of pushing people past their own created limitations.

Nikkie is a highly-recommended charismatic speaker, who provides live presentations at corporate conferences, non-profit organizations, women retreats, young girl groups, schools, and church functions.

Topics:

- *How to become a high performer*
- *Fear-fueled dreams*
- *How to live an action driven lifestyle*
- *Three step formula to live the life you want*
- *Eliminate low performing environments*

Book Nikkie Today!
678-631-8622

Connect with Nikkie!

@IAMNikkiePryce   Npryce.info@gmail.com   www.NikkiePryce.com

69116917R00067

Made in the USA
Columbia, SC
14 August 2019